I0756117

SALAMUN 3ALA MUSA WA HARUN ABNAA IMRAAN

سلام على موسى و هارون أبناء عمران

29:36 / 28:41

The Lost Legacies from the Sport of Kings

LEGENDARY EQUESTRIANS

By best selling author
SULTAN ZESHAN

Illustrated by
DR. LORIN CHASAR

Thundering hoofbeats pounded the track and threw up clumps of dirt. In the blink of an eye, horse after horse ran past in a blur of fur. Most jockeys used crops to hit them or their boots to kick their sides to make them run faster and faster. But one jockey was different: he leaned forward over his horse's neck, like he was talking to him. It was as if he whispered, come on, boy, let's go faster!

The people in the stands shook their heads at this strange sight. What was this rider thinking, sitting so strangely and not spurring his horse on at all? But in a flash, he broke through the crowd of his opponents and crossed the finish line. The crowd erupted with shock and excitement. The gentle jockey had won!

This remarkable rider was Abe Hawkins, but anyone who read about the race the next day would only find the name of the horse and the wealthy man who owned him. Why? The man who owned the plantation and stud farm where the racehorse was trained owned Abe Hawkins, too.

Abe was an enslaved person and under the law, he and the horses were both property.

Since he was a young boy, Abe had cared for the many horses on the farm. He brushed their coats to remove clouds of dirt and dust. He rubbed oil onto their fur to make it shine. He taught them to wear saddles and follow the directions of their riders. If a horse misbehaved or didn't perform, it could be cruelly punished. Abe knew what this was like, because it was the same for enslaved people. He had empathy for the horses and treated them with love and respect. He knew this was the best way to train them and get them to run their very best.

Abe's methods worked. The horses he trained didn't just run...they flew. Abe's horses didn't just race...they won. Regardless of the color of his skin, Abe was the best at what he did. In the world of horseracing, he worked hard to earn respect.

Other turfmen from across the state of Louisiana wanted him to train their horses and teach their jockeys how to ride like he did. How did Abe “talk to” the horses to make them run faster? Everyone wanted to know. Because Abe was an enslaved person, the plantation owner could sell or lease him to other stud farms for money. Abe didn’t have any say in this; he had to do what he was told. But no matter where he was forced to go, he worked hard to raise the horses with the speed and spirit to win.

By 1854, Abe went to work on a new plantation. One of the horses there, Lecomte, was trained by an enslaved man named Hark West. Hark told the plantation owner that if he wanted Lecomte to win, he had to get Abe to ride him.

So Abe saddled up and stood at the starting line, listening to the horses stomp and snort. Next to him was an Irishman named Gilbert Watson Patrick, whom everyone called Gilpatrick. He was riding a horse named Lexington who had never been beaten in a race. Not even once!

3...2...1...GO! The horses were off, thundering down the track. Shouts and cheers swelled from the stands for Lexington, the favorite. But Abe and Lecomte worked together and pulled ahead, running faster than fast. Whooosh! They crossed the finish line first, six lengths ahead of Lexington and Gilpatrick. Not only that, but Abe and Lecomte set a new world record. They broke the old one by six whole seconds.

Gilpatrick couldn't believe it! He and his undefeated horse had been beaten by an enslaved jockey who "talked" his horse into running faster. This could not stand! The Irishman demanded to race again. And so, Gilpatrick and Abe Hawkins became one of the very first rivalries in American sports history.

After that race, Abe Hawkins got his biggest challenge yet: to break a wild horse called The Whale. All the greatest horse trainers had tried their best to tame The Whale so he could be ridden, but nobody could even get close. The Whale was angry and fought hard. All he wanted was to be free. Deep in his soul, Abe Hawkins could understand those feelings. When The Whale bucked and kicked and snapped at other trainers' hands, Abe had empathy for him.

Abe walked up to the untrainable horse, slowly and calmly, with compassion. They looked into each other's eyes. Could Abe put a hand on The Whale's velvety nose? Could Abe slip a bridle over his muzzle and ears? Could Abe climb up onto his back without being thrown off? It took weeks of building trust and respect, but soon Abe had trained the untrainable horse. The racing community gave him the name, The Wise Sage of Louisiana.

In 1861, the Civil War broke out between the Union states, in the North, and the Confederate states, in the South. The Confederate states seceded from the United States soon after Abraham Lincoln became president because they knew he wanted to end the practice of slavery. The owners of the plantations and stud farms in the South did not want to give up the enslaved people who worked their land and cared for their animals without being paid. As the war raged on, Abraham Lincoln made an executive order called The Emancipation Proclamation that said all enslaved people in the Confederate states were legally free.

Abe Hawkins escaped the plantation he was working on and fled, right before the Union Army arrived to raid it themselves. Finally, Abe was free. He was no longer the property of a plantation owner who could lease him from one farm to another, without giving Abe a choice. Now that he could control his own path, where did Abe Hawkins go next? Most people didn't know. It was as if he simply vanished into the smoky grasslands of the Old South. But he may have gone to stay at a place called Woodburn Farm.

Woodburn Farm was a stud farm owned by a man named Robert A. Alexander. He had many enslaved people who worked hard to make his horses winners, including Ansel Williamson and Edward Brown. Ansel was a talented trainer, and his apprentice, Edward, was learning to care for the horses and to ride them as a jockey.

One of the most famous horses on the farm was Asteroid. His father was Lexington, the almost-undefeated horse that Abe had raced years before. Robert Alexander was so proud of Asteroid that he had artist Edward Troye paint a portrait made of him with the men who were responsible for raising him.

In the painting, Ansel held the racehorse's saddle and fourteen-year-old Edward, dressed in the blue-and-white colors of his jockey uniform of Woodburn farm, knelt to tie his boots.

The painting was meant to be a monument to the plantation owner's prize-winning horse. But it ensured that over a century later, people would look at Asteroid and see Ansel and Edward's faces, too.

Ansel and Edward wanted to learn everything they could from The Wise Sage of Louisiana. So Abe passed on a lifetime of wisdom about how to communicate with horses through empathy and respect.

Even though the Civil War was still tearing through the country, horse racing hadn't stopped. The 1864 Jersey Derby was an important race where both Black and white jockeys would come to compete together.

Woodburn Farm had a horse named Norfolk in the race, who had been trained by Ansel Williamson. Abe Hawkins went to compete, too. When he arrived, he came face to face with his rival: Gilpatrick. The Irishman would have his rematch after all.

Tails whipped! Hooves thundered! Fans cheered!
When the dust settled on the racetrack, Norfolk had won. Right behind came Abe, followed by a very angry Gilpatrick.

Two years later, the Civil War had ended and the Thirteenth Amendment to the Constitution had been passed, outlawing slavery in the United States. Ansel Williamson was a free man. But he continued to train racehorses at Woodburn Farm, now as an employee. He was preparing a horse named Merrill for the Travers Stakes race. He asked Wise Abe to help him.

When the day of the race came, Abe and Ansel arrived as a team. The smells of sweet hay, old leather, and mounds of manure were on the air as Abe mounted Merrill at the starting line. Then, he was off! In a matter of breathless moments, all of their dedication paid off: Abe and Merrill were the winners.

On September 25, 1866, the first ever Jerome Park Race was held in New York. Twenty thousand people came to watch, including Ulysses S. Grant, a military leader who had led the Union to victory. Even though the Civil War was over, repairing the damage between those who had fought against each other had just begun. Slavery was outlawed, but many Southern states had passed Black Codes that took away former enslaved people's rights and forced them to keep working for free.

Throughout the South, a hate group called The Ku Klux Klan had arisen, who believed that Black people were inferior to white people and threatened them with violence.

At the Jerome Park Race, white jockeys would race together with formerly enslaved Black jockeys and this attracted a lot of attention. Abe Hawkins entered the race and the audience watched him closely. Could he really be as good as people claimed? The crowd in the stands cheered in excitement and awe as Abe won the race! His victory showed people that the color of a person's skin did not define what they could achieve. After Jerome Park, Abe became the most famous jockey in the country.

Just a year after that amazing victory, Abe, the Wise Sage of Louisiana, passed away in the year 1867. He was buried overlooking the racetrack in Ashland plantation, Louisiana.

Ansel and Edward mourned the loss of their mentor and vowed to make sure Abe's knowledge and special methods lived on. They both worked at the Daniel Swigert stud farm now, where a Black horse trainer named Raleigh Colston Sr. had trained a horse named Kingfisher. Edward was going to ride Kingfisher in the Belmont Stakes race.

To prepare, Ansel taught Edward Abe's crouching riding posture and his method of guiding a horse around the track by talking to him with respect.

Many popular and talented horses were entered in the race. But Edward believed in himself and in all he had learned from Abe and Ansel. On the day of the race, Edward rode his very best and Kingfisher carried him over the finish line in first place! This made him the first Black man to win the Belmont Stakes.

Edward wanted to follow the example of his mentors and help other Black equestrians by passing on the wisdom of Abe and Ansel. Many young jockeys looked up to Edward, the man who won the Belmont Stakes.

In 1875, a wealthy businessman named Meriwether Lewis Clark Jr., named for his famous explorer grandfather, built a huge racetrack called Churchill Downs in Louisville, Kentucky and decided to host a race that would be like the thrilling competitions he'd attended in England. His race would be called the Kentucky Derby.

Edward Brown wanted to make his mark on that first derby. He met a talented young jockey named Oliver Lewis and prepared him to ride one of the horses he'd trained for the race: Aristides, who was owned by a turfman named H. Price McGrath. The plan was for Aristides to be the "rabbit": Oliver would ride him to the front of the pack to set the pace, urging the other jockeys to tire out their horses trying to keep up. Then, McGrath's better horse, Chesapeake, would come from behind to win.

On the day of the race, 10,000 people watched as Oliver and Aristides galloped down the track at top speed. They'd fought hard to keep the lead ahead of many other talented horses and jockeys, who thundered down the track at their heels.

But as the race neared the end, Chesapeake was so far behind, there was no chance the other horse could catch up. What should Oliver do? He looked to the sidelines to find McGrath, who waved him on. Go! Win!

Oliver leaned forward and coaxed Aristides on. With every stride, Abe, Ansel, and Edward were with them. They crossed the finish line two lengths in front of every other competitor! Oliver Lewis was the first jockey, Black or white, to win the Kentucky Derby.

The Kentucky Derby became the most important and high-class race in all of the South. The Derby was worth a lot of money, so powerful people took it very seriously. A young jockey named William "Billy" Walker competed the next year and finished fourth, but Meriwether Lewis Clark Jr. accused him of losing on purpose and threatened him for it. Who would work with Billy now? Edward Brown would. He had trained a horse named Baden-Baden and he asked Billy to ride him. Edward worked hard to train his new apprentice for the race.

The day of the Derby, Billy mounted Baden-Baden and was ready to do his very best to win. Standing at the starting line, there was nervous energy in the air. The horses nipped and stamped at one another so much that the race had to be delayed so they could calm down. Finally, they were off and running. A horse named Vera Cruz reared up and almost knocked his jockey off, which let a horse named Leonard take the lead.

Billy and Baden-Baden stayed with the pack of other horses right behind. As a turn in the track was coming up, Billy coaxed Baden-Baden ahead. Could they make it past Leonard, to get to the front? Yes! By the time the track straightened out, for the dash to the end, Billy and Baden-Baden were in the lead. They flew to the finish and William "Billy" Walker claimed his victory.

Edward had become a horse trainer everyone wanted to work with because he was patient, helpful, and talented. He was happy to pass along his knowledge to everyone he could, just like Abe and Ansel before him. Edward kept training horses and those horses kept winning. In the year 1881, he won fifty-three races.

Edward wanted to start his own business as a turfman, but he didn't have enough money to compete with white turfmen, who could spend more to help their horses win. But Edward refused to give up. Instead, he made a new plan. He used the money he did have to buy young horses, then trained them to be winners and sold them to wealthy owners who would race them. This earned him success and wealth.

In 1893, Edward took Monrovia, a horse he owned and trained, to the Kentucky Oaks race. He had worked hard with Monrovia, training him just as Abe and Ansel had taught him. But it was a dangerous time. The Ku Klux Klan was strong in the South and rules called the Jim Crow Laws segregated Black and white people, making it hard for Black people to do things like vote, find housing, or get a job. Black jockeys and owners were threatened and bullied. Still, Edward was determined and watched with pride as Monrovia won the race. No matter how angry people were to see him succeed, he held on to his dignity.

When Edward Brown passed away, newspapers wrote that his death was a great loss for American horseracing. Not only was he a talented jockey and horse trainer, he was a true role model and mentor who had spent his life lifting up others. Abe Hawkins and Ansel Williamson had put their passion, dedication, and knowledge into teaching him. He knew that he had to pass on that gift to others, keeping alive the achievements of the men who came before him.

The Sport of Kings belongs to all of them.

MEET THE LEGENDARY EQUESTRIANS

ABE HAWKINS (UNKNOWN-1867)

Abe Hawkins was born into slavery in Mississippi. He grew up on Duncan Farrar Kenner's Ashland Plantation in southern Louisiana. Over the course of his career, Hawkins earned many great victories. His first win came at a track in Paterson, New Jersey, that had no name. He was also known as the Wise Sage of Louisiana, the Slayer of Lexington, and Uncle Abe.

In 1866, Abe won the first Jerome Stakes in Queens, New York. He also won the Travers Stakes in Saratoga in 1866, riding a horse trained by Ansel Williamson named Merrill. Abe became well known in the racing industry for his extraordinary ability to communicate with horses. At the end of his life, he returned to Ashland and died there in 1867. He is buried at the racetrack and a plaque is at the entrance commemorating his life and legacy. Abe Hawkins was inducted into the Louisiana Racing Museum Hall of Fame in 1997.

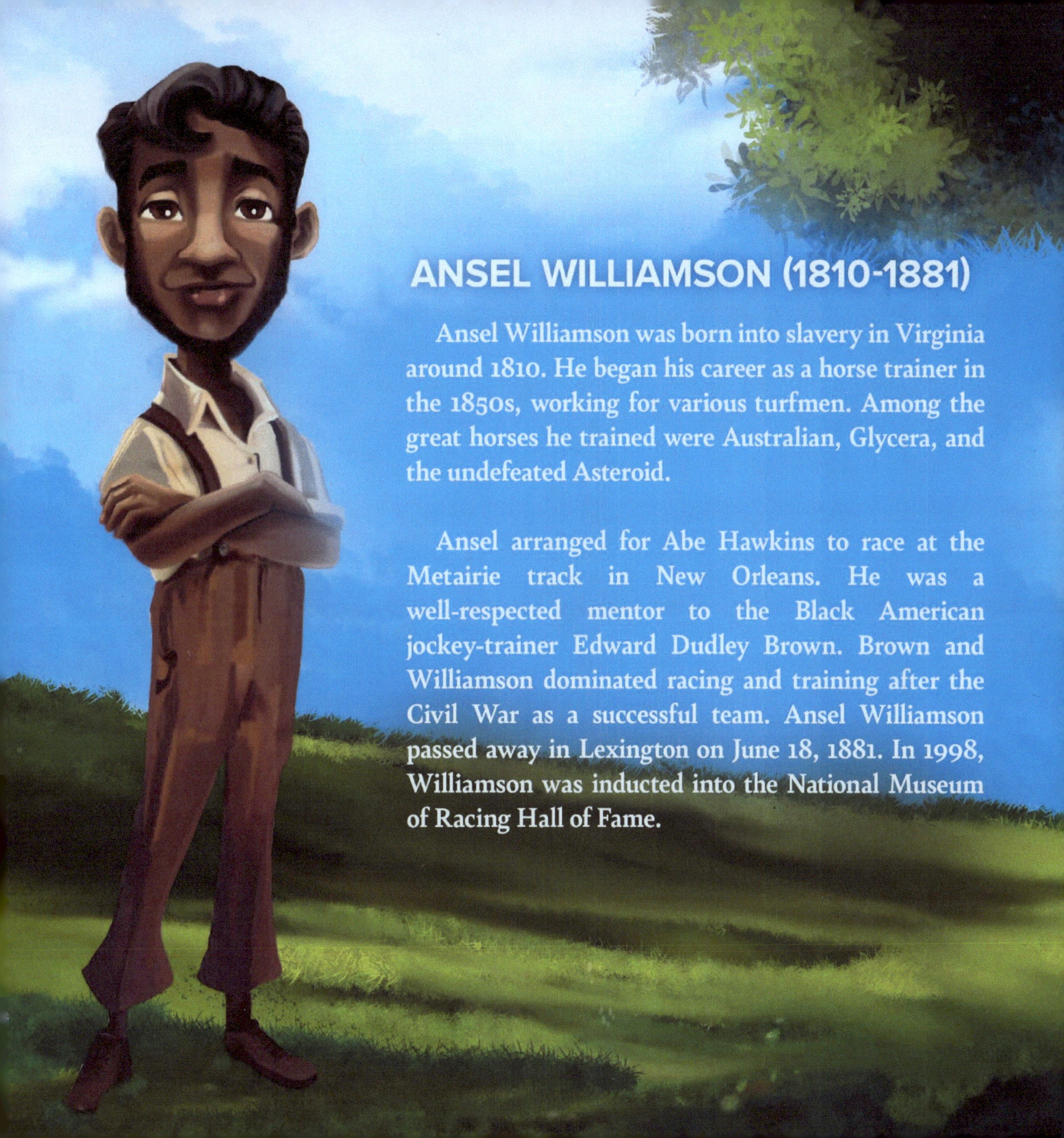

ANSEL WILLIAMSON (1810-1881)

Ansel Williamson was born into slavery in Virginia around 1810. He began his career as a horse trainer in the 1850s, working for various turfmen. Among the great horses he trained were Australian, Glycera, and the undefeated Asteroid.

Ansel arranged for Abe Hawkins to race at the Metairie track in New Orleans. He was a well-respected mentor to the Black American jockey-trainer Edward Dudley Brown. Brown and Williamson dominated racing and training after the Civil War as a successful team. Ansel Williamson passed away in Lexington on June 18, 1881. In 1998, Williamson was inducted into the National Museum of Racing Hall of Fame.

EDWARD DUDLEY BROWN
(1850-1906)

Edward Dudley Brown, also known as "Brown Dick," was born into slavery 1850, during the pre-Civil War era. He was sold to Robert A. Alexander at the age of seven. During his time at the Woodburn Estate horse farm, Edward gained an extensive knowledge of thoroughbreds and the racing industry.

Brown rode many well-known horses including Merrill, Bayswater, Kingfisher, and Vergil. In 1870, he won the Belmont Stakes on Kingfisher. Edward eventually began training horses. After leaving Robert Alexander's stables, he moved to Daniel Swigert's horse farm. One of Edward's early achievements as a trainer was training the third Kentucky Derby winner, racehorse Baden-Baden. As an owner and trainer, Brown won his second Kentucky Derby with Ben Brush in 1896. He also trained another Kentucky Derby winner, a racehorse named Plaudit. In 1906, Brown passed away. He was inducted into the National Museum of Racing's Hall of Fame in 1984.

OLIVER LEWIS (1856-1926)

Oliver Lewis was the first jockey—Black or white—to win the Kentucky Derby, at the inaugural race in May of 1875, riding Aristides. He married Lucy Wright at Mt. Gilead Baptist Church in Lexington, Kentucky, and they had several children. His parents were Goodson and Eleanor Lewis. In 2010, after a citywide road naming contest was held in Lexington, Kentucky, Oliver's name won. The connector road is called Oliver Lewis Way.

WILLIAM "BILLY" WALKER (1860-1933)

Born in Kentucky in 1860, William "Billy" Walker started racing horses at age eleven. In 1873, he amazed all with two stakes wins. In the 1875 Kentucky Derby, he finished fourth alongside Black jockeys, riding Bob Woolley. The next year, he came eighth aboard Bombay. His peak was in 1877, winning the Kentucky Derby on Baden-Baden. In 1878, he triumphed against Mollie McCarty, famed in the folk song 'Molly and Tenbrooks.' His horse lineage expertise made him sought after by horse owners. In 1891, he married Hannah at Isaac Murphy's house in Louisville, concluding his equestrian career as a Churchill Downs clocker.

TIMELINE

1856
On December 22nd the birth of Oliver Lewis, a Black jockey who went on to win the inaugural Kentucky Derby.

1861
Abraham Lincoln, who was from Kentucky, becomes the sixteenth President of the United States after winning the election. The Civil War begins.

1864
At age 14, Edward Dudley Brown wins aboard Asteroid, painted by Edward Troye with trainer Ansel Williamson. In the Jersey Derby, Ansel Williamson's horse ridden by Abe Hawkins wins.

1865
The Civil War ends, and the Thirteenth Amendment bans slavery in the United States. However, states quickly impose Black Codes to exploit Black Americans, denying them rights and compelling unpaid labor.

1875
Oliver Lewis, a jockey who was trained by Edward Brown, rides Aristides, a horse Ansel Williamson had trained, and wins the very first Kentucky Derby. He is only nineteen years old.

1877
Another of Edward Brown's apprentices, William "Billy" Walker, rides a horse named Baden-Baden in the Kentucky Derby and wins.

1881
Horses trained by Edward Brown win fifty-three races in a single year. Ansel Williamson passes away.

1896
The United States Supreme Court makes a decision in a case called Plessy v.s. Ferguson says segregation by race is legal and doesn't violate the Fourteenth Amendment as long as the accommodations are "equal."

TIMELINE

1866
Abe Hawkins wins the third Travers Stakes on Merrill, trained by Ansel Williamson. In the same year, he triumphs in the first-ever Jerome Park Race in New York, attended by Ulysses S. Grant.

1870
The Fifteenth Amendment passes, granting Black Americans voting rights, but widespread restrictive laws often make it challenging or impossible in practice. In the same year, Edward Brown makes history as the first Black man to win the Belmont Stakes riding Kingfisher.

1872
Meriweather Lewis Clark Jr. arrives in America from Liverpool, England, after attending the Epsom Derby. He leases 80 acres of land from uncles John and Henry Churchill, initiating the construction of Churchill Downs racetrack and establishing The Jockey Club

1874
Edward Brown becomes a horse trainer and mentor to other jockeys. First public notice of the racetrack called Churchill Downs in the Courier Journal.

1906
Edward Dudley Brown passes away.

1984
Edward Dudley Brown is inducted into the prestigious National Museum Racing Hall of Fame.

1997
Abe Hawkins is inducted into Louisiana's prestigious Fair Grounds Racing Hall of Fame in New Orleans.

1998
Ansel Williamson is inducted into the prestigious National Museum Racing Hall of Fame.

GLOSSARY

Apprentice: A person who is learning a specific job or craft from a skilled professional.

Black Codes: Laws passed in the South immediately following the abolishment of slavery that ensured Black Americans could continue to be forced to work for free in many cases and also severely restricted their rights and freedoms.

Civil War: A war in which a country breaks apart and fights against itself. In the United States, the North, known as the Union, fought against the South, known as the Confederacy, from 1861-1865.

Derby: An annual race reserved for three-year-old horses.

Emancipation Proclamation: An executive order made by Abraham Lincoln on January 1, 1863 that said all enslaved people in the Confederate states were officially free under the law. The problem was, the Confederacy did not consider themselves part of the United States anymore, nor did they consider Abraham Lincoln to be their president. So enslaved people could only gain this freedom if they escaped their enslavers and fled to the Union states or were freed by the Union army.

Equestrian: A person who rides horses. Can also be used to describe anything that relates to horseback riding.

Jim Crow Era: A post-Civil War era in which anti-Black laws in the United States were enforced to ensure that Black Americans were treated as second class citizens and segregated, or separated, from white Americans.

Jockey: A person whose job is to ride horses in races.

Ku Klux Klan: A white supremacist, terrorist, hate group in the United States that was started by white Protestant men who were former Confederates. They promote violence against minorities including Black Americans, Jewish people, Asian Americans, Latinx Americans, Native Americans, Catholics, and many more.

GLOSSARY

Lease: A contract where one person allows someone else to use their property for a set amount of time for a sum of money. In this case, plantation owners could lease their enslaved people who had desirable skills to other plantation owners for a certain amount of time to make extra money.

Length: A measure of the distance between horses in a race, often used to describe how far the second-place horse was behind the winner. It counts the number of horses that could fit between the two contestants. One "length" is typically 8-9 feet, depending on the size of the horse being used to measure.

Plantation: An estate including farmland that is worked by laborers who live on the land. Before the Civil War, these workers would have been enslaved people.

StudFarm: A farm where race horses are bred and trained.

Turfman: A person who owns or trains racehorses and is passionate about the sport.

Secede: To formally leave or withdraw from membership in a group or larger body. During the Civil War, the South seceded from the United States of America. They did not want to be part of the country anymore and tried to form their own, called the Confederate States of America.

Thirteenth Amendment: This amendment to the constitution, ratified in 1865, abolished slavery and involuntary servitude throughout the United States, except as punishment for a crime.

Stakes: A race in which part of the prize money is offered by the owners of the horses who enter. Their money is in the pot for the winner, so they have a "stake" in the result of the race.

Thoroughbred: A type of horse bred specifically for horseracing. These horses only have ancestry from English mares and Arabian stallions and are known for being good at racing and jumping.

AUTHOR'S NOTE

Creating *Legendary Equestrians*: The Lost Legacies from the Sport of Kings has been a wonderful adventure for me, as I am a big fan of horses and history. This book is a special tribute to amazing people who made a huge difference in the world of horse racing. My time studying at Louisiana State University inspired me a lot, especially learning about Abe Hawkins. Abe was a superstar jockey from Baton Rouge, Louisiana, the same place where I grew up! He had a special connection with horses and changed the sport in big ways.

Legendary Equestrians is like a colorful doorway into the exciting stories of horse racing pioneers. It shines a light on parts of our history that many people don't know about. The book also celebrates heroes like Ansel Williamson and Edward Brown. They faced many tough challenges but still made important contributions to horse racing with their bravery and skill. But this book is not just about the past. It's also here to inspire readers to dream big and work hard. It shows that with talent, never giving up, and hard work, anyone can overcome challenges and reach their goals, no matter how tough they seem. Think of Legendary Equestrians as a bright guiding light, showing young readers the way to their dreams, reminding them that anything is possible. With a strong spirit and a never-quit attitude, they too can make a big impact on the world and bravely chase their dreams.

Further Reading for Kids About Slavery, the Civil War, and Reconstruction:

The 1619 Project: Born on the Water by Nikole Hannah-Jones and Renée Watson, illustrated by Nikkolas Smith
All Different Now: Juneteenth, the First Day of Freedom by Angela Johnson, illustrated by E.B. Lewis
The Amazing Age of John Roy Lynch by Chris Barton, illustrated by Don Tate
Freedom Over Me: Eleven Slaves, Their Lives and Dreams Brought to Life by Ashley Bryan
Hammering for Freedom by Rita Lorraine Hubbard, illustrated by John Holyfield
Heart and Soul: The Story of America and African Americans by Kadir Nelson
Henry's Freedom Box by Ellen Levine, illustrated by Kadir Nelson

Dedicated to the cherished memory of my grandmother, the late Virgie Ezelle Patton, a gifted artist known for her luminous portraits and dancelike depictions of Black women in states of freedom and transcendence, and to the Legendary Black Equestrians of American horse racing, whose stories are celebrated and brought to life through this work.
- Dr. Lorin Chasar

Published in the United States by Project Equestrian X - Legendary Maestros LLC.

For permissions, contact: Email: projectequestrianx@gmail.com
Typography & Design: Safeer Ahmed copyright © 2023 by Sultan Zeshan
Editor: Sarah Jane Abbott

Library of Congress Control Number: 2023918173
IDENTIFIERS: LCCN (2023918173) (print) | LCCN (2023918173) (eBook)
| ISBN 978-1-959210-05-4 (hardcover) |
| ISBN 978-1-959210-06-1 (paperback) | ISBN 978-1-959210-07-8 (eBook)
| ASIN B0C8V6BW83 (Kindle)
Printed in the U.S.A. | FIRST EDITION

www.ingramcontent.com/pod-product-compliance
Lightning Source LLC
LaVergne TN
LVHW070155110826
845147LV00002B/403
* 9 7 8 1 9 5 9 2 1 0 0 6 1 *